The Ugly Truth About Tithes

The Greatest Church Manipulation

by Michael B Cobb Jr

CONTENTS

Contents

Preface

As I sit here, pen in hand, I am compelled to take you on a deep dive into one of the most hotly debated topics within the Christian faith—the practice of tithing. It is a matter that has swirled around the hallowed halls of churches, igniting fierce discussions and, at times, deep-seated animosities among the faithful. For too long, the subject of tithes has been enshrouded in layers of misunderstanding, manipulation, and fear, leading many well-meaning individuals to support institutions—not out of faith but out of obligation. In this book, "The Ugly Truth About Tithes," we peel back the layers, exposing the historical context, scriptural implications, and moral quandaries surrounding this controversial practice. With an open heart and inquisitive spirit, I invite you to join me on this journey of revelation, questioning, and empowerment, a voyage designed not only to inform but also to liberate.

From the earliest days of the Israelites, tithing was deeply embedded in their covenant with God, a concept that promised blessings in return for offerings given as a part of their communal and spiritual identity. However, as we traverse through the ages and into contemporary settings, we unearth a startling transformation—

one in which tithing has morphed into an expectation that lodges itself deeply in the lives of unsuspecting followers of Christ, accompanied by the admonitions of church leaders who wield scripture like a weapon. It is an alarming reality that suggests our faith, which should gracefully nurture us, is sometimes twisted into a vehicle for compliance, demanding our wallets along with our souls. As such, the central theme of this exploration becomes glaringly obvious: the manipulation of faith for financial gain, where fear supplants genuine spirituality and love.

What would it look like to walk away from the shackles of obligatory giving? Imagine a world where followers of Christ are not measured by the weight of their wallets but instead nurtured by the content of their hearts. "The Ugly Truth About Tithes" is not merely an exposé; it is a call to action. It urges you, dear reader, to challenge the narrative you have been told—a narrative woven with mistruths that hinge on coercion and fear, and built upon a misunderstanding of scriptural teachings. We embark on an exploration of the New Testament's relative silence on tithing, spotlighting the pivotal absence of explicit directives, which raises profound questions about compliance versus genuine generosity. Are we as Christians truly bound by a law that no longer applies, or are we free to embrace a richer, more fulfilling expression of love through voluntary giving? The very fabric of our financial interactions with the church calls for scrutiny, and it is time to take a courageous step toward clarity and enlightenment.

Within these pages, you will find stories not only mine, but the poignant experiences of many whose lives have been altered by the manipulation that comes under the banner of spirituality. Their journeys highlight the psychological toll that fear-driven compliance can unleash, shattering relationships and tainting the sacred experience of worship. This exploration aims to lay bare how such tactics erode genuine spiritual connections. Imagine feeling that your financial status is the sole measure of your faith—what an insidious notion! It can cause even the most devout believers to spiral into doubt and shame when they cannot meet the expectations set forth by church leaders, who often mishandle scriptural teachings to bolster their authority and financial security.

As we reach beyond the harsh realities of manipulative practices, we shall also illuminate the vital importance of community and generosity, which serve as the lifeblood of a thriving church. We will delve into the beautiful alternative of voluntary giving, examining how it can create a spirit of openness and trust, nurturing relationships within congregations rather than driving wedges of guilt or fear. A church should not merely be a place where monetary commitment is prioritized over emotional and spiritual support; rather, it should emerge as a sanctuary, rich with understanding, love, and generosity.

Ultimately, "The Ugly Truth About Tithes" invites you to take a step back and reflect. It is not merely about uncovering truths; it is about how you choose to shape your own journey with faith and finances. Encouraging you to envision a paradigm where monetary contributions are rooted in love rather than obligation, the book seeks to arm you with the tools to redefine what giving means in your life. We will walk together through the vital steps necessary to demand accountability from those who shepherd their flocks, reinforcing the need for transparency and integrity in church funding. As you explore these chapters, I hope you find not only the courage to challenge inherited beliefs but also the empowerment that comes from reclaiming your narrative—a narrative marked not by obligation but by flourishing relationships and a renewed sense of spiritual connection.

So let us embark on this journey together, where challenging conversations, introspective reflections, and newfound freedoms await. In a world often fraught with confusion, fear, and manipulation, we have the power to rewrite our stories—stories that celebrate love, community, and above all, faith liberated from financial coercion. Welcome to "The Ugly Truth About Tithes." May it spark within you the courage and conviction to seek, ask, and dare to believe in a new way of living and giving. Your journey awaits.

Chapter One

The Origins of Tithing

What is Tithing?

Tithing, at its most fundamental level, refers to the practice of giving one-tenth of one's income or produce, historically rooted in a covenantal relationship between God and His people, particularly within the Old Testament narrative. This act of worship was not merely a financial transaction; instead, it served as a tangible expression of trust and gratitude towards God, reinforcing a communal identity and an acknowledgment of divine providence. The origins of tithing can be traced back to the laws given to the Israelites, where it was enshrined in the books of Leviticus, Numbers, and Deuteronomy, illustrating both a spiritual discipline and a societal mechanism that ensured the sustenance of the priestly tribe, the Levites. In a covenant structured by mutual obligations, God promised to be their protector and provider, while the Israelites were instructed to honor Him with their first fruits and a portion of their land's yield, thereby establishing a cycle of blessing rooted in obedience. This was not just a duty, but a profound connection that fostered gratitude and acknowledged dependence on a higher power. Tithing, therefore, was deeply interwoven with the agricultural calendar of the Israelites, intimately linked to their cycles of planting and harvesting, reinforcing the understanding that all they had came as a gift from God. The act of tithing was also meant to promote equity within the community, as the Levites, who had no land of their own, relied entirely on the tithes of the people for their sustenance, serving as a reminder of the collective responsibility to care for those who served in spiritual leadership. In many ways, this practice reflected the socio-economic conditions of ancient Israel, focusing on community and shared worship rather than individual self-interest. The significance of tithing went beyond the physical gift— it became a public declaration of allegiance to God, symbolizing a commitment to live according to His commands and trust in His provision. It was a way for the Israelites to remain connected to their divine covenant, reinforcing the idea that their relationship with God was reciprocal, flourishing within a system grounded in loyalty, reverence, and shared blessings. Understanding this historical context is vital for grasping the subsequent evolution of the tithing concept, especially as it transitioned into contemporary interpretations that are often devoid of the rich theological and communal meanings that defined its initial practice among the ancient Israelites.

Biblical Foundations

In the Old Testament, the concept of tithing emerges prominently as a practice deeply woven into the fabric of Israelite society and its relationship with God. It is essential to understand that tithing was not merely a financial obligation but a critical aspect of the covenant between the Israelites and Yahweh. Tithes were seen as a way to acknowledge God's sovereignty over one's wealth and to express gratitude for the many blessings bestowed upon them. The primary scriptural references to tithing can be found in books such as Leviticus, Numbers, and Deuteronomy, where the Israelites were commanded to set aside a tenth of their harvest and livestock **(not money)** for the Levitical priests and for festivals dedicated to worship.

To tithe today according to biblical principles would be more around 23.3%. There were three types of tithes. **The Levitical Tithe** which was the tithe of everything from the land. This first 10% was given to support the Levites that served in the temple. This was to be given *annually*. The second tithe was **The Festival Tithe**. This too was 10% for religious festivals and celebrations. The giver and their family were to enjoy this tithe as a way to rejoice and fellowship with God's people *annually*. God told the Israelites to eat the tithe of their flock, grain, and herds in the presence of the Lord. During the festival if they had to travel and they could not carry their tithe because it was to far, then they could exchange it for silver. This was the only time the monetary concept was mentioned. It was to buy what they could not carry once they reached their destination. The third tithe was **The Poor Tithe** which was approximately around 3.3%. This was a charity tithe given for the widows, orphans, and the needy every three years to support and care for them. These allocations served practical purposes, ensuring that those who dedicated their lives to serving God through the priesthood were supported as well as those in need, thereby fostering a spiritual order essential for communal worship and relationship with God. This was not based merely on a transactional understanding of divine favor but rather rooted in a communal obligation; the tithe represented a shared commitment to the covenant community, strengthening bonds among the people as they collectively honored God.

The origins of tithing are perhaps best illustrated in Genesis chapter 14 when Abraham WILLINGLY gave a tithe to Melchizedek, the king of Salem and priest of God Most High, after his victory over King Kedorlaomer. This act of giving a *tenth of his spoils* symbolizes recognition of God's authority and blessings in his life. Furthermore, the Mosaic Law reiterates this concept as the Israelites were commanded to celebrate the Feast of Weeks by bringing a tithe of the harvest to the place where God chose to put His name, emphasizing the importance of remembering God's provision during times of celebration and gratitude. Again, in Deuteronomy, tithing is coupled with a call to care for the marginalized, as it is written that the tithes are to be shared with the Levites, the foreigners, the orphans, and the widows, thus reinforcing the societal role of the tithe as a means to promote justice, compassion, and community support, while also fostering a sense of divine accountability among the Israelites.

As we delve deeper into the scriptural text, we begin to recognize the rich tapestry of cultural and spiritual significance tithing held for the Israelites. It illustrated their identity as a chosen people, as the act of giving was tied to their very status as inhabitants of a covenant relationship with Yahweh. They understood that all that they possessed was a gift from God, and their tithes were a way of returning a portion of those gifts back to Him, symbolizing trust and reliance on His provision. In this light, tithing transcended the mundane act of giving; it became a powerful demonstration of their faith and an affirmation of God's place in their lives. The historical and theological context surrounding the practice of tithing in the Old Testament paints a vivid picture of a community striving to live in alignment with divine principles, establishing a foundation for understanding how such practices were rooted in an era vastly different from today's financial landscapes.

However, as we assess the biblical foundations of tithing, it is crucial to maintain an awareness of the evolution of these practices beyond their original intent. While those ancient laws were significant to the Israelites, it provokes thoughtful consideration of how these foundations are often misapplied in modern contexts, potentially disconnecting them from their original covenantal spirit designed to foster community and support rather than coercion or fear. The scriptures serve as a testament not only to the origination of tithing as an act of faithfulness but also to the broader call for community and compassion among God's people. As we step further into the New Testament narratives and the teachings of Jesus and His apostles, we will continue to unravel the complexities of this practice, questioning the relevance of obligatory tithing in light of the grace that the New Covenant brings and challenging ourselves to consider how the significance of our generosity can be reframed in accordance with principles of love, free will, and relational stewardship rather than the rigid mandates of law.

The Israelites and Tithing

In the ancient world of the Israelites, tithing was woven into the very fabric of their communal and spiritual existence. It was not merely a practice of financial obligation; rather, it represented a profound covenantal relationship with God, a relationship underscored by mutual faithfulness and provision. The concept of tithing can be traced back to the laws given to the Israelites, chiefly articulated in the books of Leviticus and Deuteronomy. These statutes dictated that a tenth of the **produce from the land and the livestock** be set apart, not as a burdensome tax, but as a holy offering dedicated to the Lord. This was not just a financial transaction, but a heartfelt acknowledgment of God's sovereignty and provision for their lives. The Israelites were wanderers and farmers, often reliant on uncertain harvests and the mercy of nature, so tithing served as a tangible demonstration of their trust in God's continual care and abundance.

The significance of tithing extended beyond personal spirituality; it was integral to the functioning of their society itself. The Levites, designated as the priestly class within the Israelite community, had no land of their own and were thus dependent on the tithes of the people for their livelihood. This created a system wherein the act of tithing nurtured not only the spiritual health of the community but also the practical needs of those who served God and the nation. It fostered a sense of collective responsibility and interdependence, binding the community together through shared beliefs and practices. In this covenantal economy, tithing was also a means of ensuring that those who could not provide for themselves—such as the orphans, widows, and strangers—were cared for, thus embodying the deeper ethical mandates woven throughout their scriptures.

Moreover, the act of tithing became a physical manifestation of loyalty to the covenant established at Sinai, wherein the people promised to follow God's laws in exchange for His protection and guidance. When Israelites fulfilled their tithing obligations, they engaged in a ritual that not only reminded them of their dependence on God but also reinforced their identity as a chosen people, set apart for divine purposes. It was a vibrant communal act, celebrated with feasts and shared meals which drew families and neighbors together in joy as they collectively recognized God's provision. In this way, the rhythm of tithing infused their lives with a sense of gratitude and purpose, creating a framework within which they could experience their faith viscerally and publicly.

As time passed and cultural contexts shifted, the original intent and meaning of these tithing laws saw various interpretations, yet the roots remained the same. **For the Israelites, tithing was never solely about adhering to a monetary guideline; it was about cultivating a heart posture of gratitude, stewardship, and community kinship under God's promises.** As such, understanding the role of tithing in the Israelite community is more than an academic exercise; it invites us to explore the ways in which faith, obligation, and community intertwine, ultimately shaping the spiritual identity of a people who believed that everything they had was a divine gift. Through this lens, we can begin to appreciate how far contemporary practices might stray from the original intent, prompting a reassessment of what it truly means to give in a way that honors both our relationship with the Divine and the welfare of our communities.

Chapter Two

The Silence of the New Testament

Jesus' Teachings on Money

In examining Jesus' teachings on money, we uncover a profound shift from the obligated practices of the Old Testament to a more nuanced understanding of wealth and generosity that permeates the New Testament. Central to Jesus' message is the idea that the heart of giving transcends legalistic obligations, such as the tithe, instead focusing on the motivations behind our financial actions and the spirit in which we offer our resources. One striking passage comes from the Gospel of Matthew, where Jesus challenges the rich young ruler, inviting him to sell all his possessions and give to the poor, illustrating that true discipleship requires surrendering earthly attachments for the sake of heavenly treasures. Here, wealth is portrayed not as a blessing to be hoarded, but as a responsibility to be shared, emphasizing that our relationship with money ought to reflect our commitment to love and service towards others. Jesus further underscores this principle in the Sermon on the Mount, where He teaches that one cannot serve both God and money, cleverly drawing a line between devotion to spiritual pursuits and the entrapments of materialism. The radical call to generosity is echoed in the parable of the Good Samaritan, where the act of helping others is framed as the ultimate expression of neighborly love, transcending cultural, religious, and social barriers. Through these teachings, Jesus invites His followers to embrace a lifestyle characterized by voluntary generosity, where the depth of one's compassion takes precedence over the constraints of tradition and law. Furthermore, in Luke's account, Jesus praises the widow who offered her two small coins in the temple, illustrating that it is not the amount that matters but the heart behind the gift; in God's economy, sacrificial giving born from love holds greater value than substantial contributions afforded by surplus. This narrative serves as a poignant reminder that the early church, rooted in the teachings of Christ, thrived not on the vintage practice of tithing but through communal sharing, where believers supported one another out of love, leading to the practical fulfillment of Christ's command to care for the least among them. Thus, the essence of Jesus' teachings on money emerges as an invitation to redefine our relationship with wealth, moving away from obligation and shifting towards an ethos of voluntary love — one that empowers individuals to engage with their resources not out of fear or obligation but from the overflow of their hearts, liberated to embody the generosity that reflects the very nature of the One they follow.

Paul's Letters and Giving

In examining Paul's letters, a profound shift in the understanding of financial contributions within the early church comes into focus, revealing a compelling narrative of love, generosity, and voluntary giving. Unlike the rigid and prescriptive laws surrounding tithing present in the Old Testament, the New Testament writings of Paul advocate for a much more relational and heartfelt approach to giving. In his letters to various congregations, Paul emphasizes that financial contributions should stem from a place of joy, gratitude, and a willingness to support one another, rather than out of obligation or fear of divine punishment. In 2 Corinthians 9:7, he famously declares that "each one must give as he has decided in his heart, not reluctantly or under compulsion, for God loves a cheerful giver." This scripture encapsulates the essence of Paul's teaching: giving is a personal act of the heart and spirit, deliberately chosen in the light of one's love for God and for others, free from the coercive frameworks that dominated prior traditions.

The early church, through Paul's teachings, was profoundly shaped by the understanding that their financial contributions were less about meeting a legalistic requirement and more about fostering community and sharing resources for mutual benefit. A powerful moment in this discourse occurs when Paul references the Macedonians in 2 Corinthians 8, highlighting their extraordinary generosity despite extreme poverty. He commends them not for fulfilling a numerical standard of giving, but for surpassing expectations by their heartfelt desire to support their fellow believers in need. This narrative underlines the transformative power of voluntary giving, revealing how a community fueled by love can create an environment where financial support becomes a natural outpouring of their collective faith. Paul, with his emphatic encouragement of the church in Corinth, reinforces the idea that genuine generosity flows from the blessings one has received, not from fear of scarcity or divine retribution.

Furthermore, in Galatians 6:2, Paul urges believers to "bear one another's burdens, and so fulfill the law of Christ," making it abundantly clear that support for one another extends beyond mere financial contribution. It invites an ethos of love, compassion, and solidarity, marking a significant departure from the transactional mentality often associated with tithing. This shift evokes an inspiring vision wherein the act of giving intertwines with the very fabric of mutual care and empowerment, inspiring church members to contribute in ways that resonate with their personal circumstances and convictions.

Even as Paul addresses the need for financial support for church leaders, he does so in a manner that underscores the importance of respect and mutuality in these relationships. In 1 Timothy 5:17-18, he discusses the significance of compensating those who labor in preaching and teaching, yet this instruction is rooted in acknowledging the worth of their contributions rather than enforcing a compulsory tax on the followers of Christ. The overarching message is clear: the New Testament writers sought to cultivate community-driven relationships where giving was not bound by oppressive rules, but encouraged in the spirit of freedom, love, and the shared mission of the church.

The contrast between these teachings and the practice of tithing highlights a critical realization for contemporary believers. The lack of direct admonitions or examples enforcing a rigid tithing practice in Paul's letters invites individuals to reassess their current financial obligations to the church critically. Instead of feeling entrapped by financial guilt or fear, readers are encouraged to reclaim their personal agency in how they contribute, reinstating the principles of love and generosity that echo throughout Paul's epistles. The early church thrived not on the fear of curses or the expectation of rigid adherence to a set percentage but through the heartfelt and willing participation of its members, each contributing as they felt led, perfectly illustrating that financial contributions within the body of Christ should flow from the spirit of community and grace rather than obligation or manipulation. Ultimately, Paul's letters invite a powerful reimagining of giving, one characterized not by strings attached or burdens imposed, but by the profound joy of sharing one's gifts for the betterment of others, thereby fostering a rich tapestry of support and mutual care within the Christian community. Through this lens, the possibility of financial freedom and spiritual fulfillment emerges, culminating in an empowered congregation capable of redefining what it means to give within a community of faith.

The Early Church Practices

In the vibrant communities of the early church, the spirit of generosity was cultivated as a natural expression of faith rather than an obligatory duty. The followers of Jesus, motivated by love and a collective sense of purpose, shared their resources, ensuring that no one among them lacked anything essential. As illustrated in the book of Acts, the early Christians demonstrated a radical approach to communal living, where possessions were pooled together, and believers were encouraged to sell their own land or houses as necessary to meet the needs of others. This profound commitment to one another was not born from a mandate but emerged from the joyous understanding of shared identity in Christ, which rendered individual material possessions secondary to the communal good. The Apostle Paul, in his letters, often emphasized this ethos of giving, urging his readers to give cheerfully and generously. In 2 Corinthians, he extols the virtues of a generous heart and points out that each believer should determine in their heart what to give, emphasizing that the act of giving should stem from personal conviction and desire, not compulsion. This highlights the absence of rigid tithing laws; instead, the community thrived on voluntary contributions fueled by love and mutual concern. The early Christians did not measure their worth by the percent of income given, but rather by the spirit behind their gifts and the impact on their brothers and sisters within the faith community. The practice of financial support in these early gatherings was a stark contrast to contemporary tithing pressures seen in many modern churches today; instead, members were invited to respond to the needs of the community as they felt led, thus establishing an environment rich in trust, compassion, and understanding. This voluntary principle, pivoting away from the fear-infused mandates of legalism, fostered an atmosphere where generosity flowed freely and naturally, serving as a testament to their faith in God's provision and the beauty of interdependence. The early church, therefore, stands as a remarkable example of a community energized by love, a model of financial support that should inspire current and future generations to reconsider the very foundations of their giving practices and reframe the relationship between faith and finances in a more liberating and affirming light.

Chapter Three

Manipulating Scripture

Quotes Taken Out of Context

In the vast tapestry of biblical interpretation, nothing is quite as potent—or as dangerous—as the selective quotation of scripture. This practice, often employed by church leaders to underpin their doctrines, has the uncanny ability to twist the very essence of scriptural teachings into fear-laden mandates. Followers of Christ, at the intersection of faith and financial obligation, frequently find themselves ensnared in a web of misinterpretations, often perpetuated by those who should be shepherding them towards a deeper understanding of the divine but instead manipulate texts to serve their agendas. A glaring example of this phenomenon is the pervasive use of Malachi 3:10, which proclaims, "Bring all the tithes into the storehouse, that there may be food in My house." Immediately, this verse is wielded as a weapon, a rallying cry urging parishioners to adhere to tithing under the guise of divine commandment. Yet, stripped of its historical context, this scripture is often used to conjure up imagery of impending curses for noncompliance—"You're robbing God!" They are told, with a gravity as if the heavens themselves hinge on their monetary contributions. In reality, this passage emerges from a narrative rooted in an ancient agricultural society where the context of sacrifice and sustenance takes precedence over mere financial obligation. The selection of such verses, devoid of thorough exploration of their meaning within the broader biblical narrative, paints an incomplete picture, capturing the hearts and wallets of individuals while distorting the loving and grace-filled essence of biblical teachings.

Moreover, the practice of cherry-picking verses is not confined to the Old Testament; contemporary church leaders have also misappropriated passages from the New Testament, claiming that Jesus Himself spoke unequivocally about the necessity of tithing. One prominent example, Matthew 23:23, which admonishes the Pharisees for their meticulous tithing of herbs while neglecting weightier matters of the law—justice, mercy, and faithfulness—is often misread as an endorsement of tithing rather than a critique of hollow religious observance. This selective interpretation overlooks the profound moral lesson embedded within the text; instead, it emphasizes a narrow physical obedience to financial giving, overshadowing the intent to foster a heart of generosity and compassion in the community. This is the essence of manipulation—wringing from scripture a semblance of support for practices that prioritize financial gain over spiritual development. Followers of Christ, many of whom enter church with genuine intentions, often find their faith exploited, their understanding of scriptural teachings eroded. They are led to believe that their worthiness before God hinges solely on their ability to contribute financially, creating an insidious cycle of compliance steeped in fear. By scrutinizing these misquoted scriptures and understanding their original intent within the multifaceted landscape of biblical teachings, individuals can begin to disentangle their financial obligations from their spiritual worth, paving the way toward a more liberated, enlightened understanding of both faith and finances, free from the shackles of manipulation that have plagued so many. The road ahead lies in reclaiming the joy of giving, guided not by fear, but by love and genuine generosity that aligns with the heart of the gospel itself. It is imperative, then, that followers of Christ learn to discern the truth of scripture from the distortions that seek to bind them, fostering a healthier, transparent dialogue about what it truly means to live generously in both spirit and substance.

Fear Tactics in the Pulpit

In many contemporary churches, an unsettling pattern emerges during sermons that delve into the topic of tithing. A particular brand of rhetoric is employed—one that embraces fear as a mechanism to compel the faithful into financial compliance. These sermons often start with an innocuous enough premise, perhaps a story of generosity or a reflection on God's blessings, but gradually shift to a more sinister warning. The underlying subtext is clear: failure to give, particularly in the context of the prescribed ten percent tithe, will not only curtail spiritual blessings but could also lead to dire consequences. This manipulation finds its roots in misquoted scripture—passages taken out of context to serve the needs of the speaker rather than the intended message. For instance, references to Malachi 3:10, where God challenges the Israelites to bring the full tithe into the storehouse, are frequently delivered with an air of foreboding about robbing God, an unsettling phrase that reverberates in the minds of followers of Christ long after the service ends. The implication is that neglecting to tithe is not merely a financial oversight, but a significant spiritual transgression stirred by Biblical admonishment.

Moreover, such fear tactics are often reinforced by compelling stories of individuals who supposedly faced catastrophic failures after failing to tithe. These anecdotes, while they might hold a kernel of truth in individual experiences, are employed selectively to create a narrative of inevitable ruin. Followers of Christ are left with a prevailing dread: failing to give as instructed could lead to divine retribution, illness, or unwarranted financial burdens. This psychological manipulation breeds further reliance on the church and its teachings, entrenching members in a cycle of fear and compliance. It is not uncommon for these sermons to evince a sense of urgency—calls to action that create a pressure cooker atmosphere: "You must act now, lest you be cursed!" This strategy exploits the innate human desire for security—a desire that is easily twisted into the belief that only through compliance can one secure a favorable outcome in life.

Furthermore, the inclusion of personal testimonies from the pulpit, where church leaders recount miraculous financial turnarounds tied directly to faithful tithing, captures the imagination. These narratives serve an even greater purpose: they operate like parables, reinforcing the rules of a financial belief system that many followers of Christ are already predisposed to accept. Like cautionary tales, these testimonies weave a narrative that positions tithing not merely as a guideline, but as a non-negotiable covenant between the faithful and their Creator. This rhetoric crescendos into a climax of emotional urgency, where the message is unmistakably clear: to deny the church, your tithe is to play games with your very salvation and financial stability.

All of these elements culminate in a construct where psychological and spiritual coercion leave little room for critical thought or personal agency. The manipulation of scriptural teachings may not simply be an oversight; it is a methodical approach to maintaining control over a congregation that, out of fear, may willingly surrender their financial autonomy. This exchange, cloaked under the guise of divine expectation, transforms the act of giving into an obligatory movement, one that ties the heart's intention and spiritual commitment to a contracted obedience defined by dollar amounts rather than genuine generosity. The implications extend beyond the individual to the very fabric of community life; as church funding increasingly relies on such fear-laden tactics, discussions regarding financial ethics and stewardship are suppressed, leaving congregations to operate under a veil of silence propelled by the specter of judgment and reprisal. Thus, the psychological ramifications of fear tactics in the pulpit not only harm individual relationships with God but also undermine the entire notion of community and generosity that should ideally underpin a church's mission.

The Curse of the Tithe

Within the walls of many churches, an insidious doctrine has permeated the teachings on financial contributions, feeding a powerful narrative that not tithing invites divine curses or leads one into a state of perpetual poverty. This notion has been meticulously crafted by church leaders who, whether intentionally or through a misguided interpretation of scripture, propagate the idea that falling short in tithes equates to falling short of God's blessings. They deftly wield verses such as Malachi 3:8-10, which states that withholding the tithe is akin to robbing God, and they assert that this theft brings upon the faithful a curse. With a flourish, they paint a dire picture of what it means not to give, warning followers of Christ that financial ruin, unfulfilled dreams, and spiritual desolation await those who fail to comply with the stringent demands of tithing. This narrative can turn what should be a personal journey of faith into a fear-laden obligation where the concept of God's providence is twisted into a transactional relationship, one that safeguards blessings only for those willing to empty their pockets.

Leaders often employ emotional techniques during sermons, recounting compelling anecdotes woven with their personal experiences of financial breakthrough tied to their tithing practices. The congregation is led to believe that their wealth and success are directly correlated with their percentage contributions to the church. Bound by a blend of fear and guilt, individuals may find themselves in a cycle where their financial decisions are dictated not by personal calling or genuine willingness, but by the looming dread of spiritual repercussions instilled by their leaders. The irony here is palpable; what should be an uplifting and liberating act of giving is morphed into a manipulative tool that some use to exert control over their congregation. Additional misquoted scriptures are threaded throughout these teachings, carefully chosen to help maintain this framework, leaving followers of Christ anxious about their standing within the community and their relationship with God, often dictating their entire financial behavior in an unhealthy manner.

Moreover, tales of testimonies are shared, showcasing individuals who supposedly experienced miraculous financial blessings after committing themselves to tithing. These heartfelt stories serve to further entrench the belief that divine favor is contingent upon one's monetary contributions. It creates a dichotomy where givers are celebrated, and non-givers are looked upon with suspicion, or even worse, pity. This manipulation can lead members to neglect their financial responsibilities outside the church, as they funnel funds away from family needs and humanitarian causes, believing their primary obligation lies exclusively with the church.

In promoting this fear-based model, church leaders overlook the fundamental principles of generosity and community that permeate the Scriptures. They fail to teach that true giving should stem from a place of love and gratefulness rather than compulsion and dread; it ought to resonate with a believer's unique relationship with God and their community. Many fail to grasp that the New Testament does not mandate tithing as an obligation but instead calls for a spirit of generosity and cheerfulness in giving, highlighting the abundant grace bestowed upon believers rather than punitive repercussions for failing to fulfill a law. These misinterpretations keep followers of Christ tethered to a worn-out doctrine, preventing them from experiencing the transformative joy that comes with making one's own financial choices in alignment with their values, fostering a deeper and more authentic relationship with both faith and finances. In this stifling environment, a plea for liberation arises, harkening a time for believers to reclaim their understanding of stewardship, a journey away from manipulative teachings toward a refreshing embrace of generous, unforced giving rooted in love rather than fear.

Chapter Four

The Psychological Impact

Testimonies of Fear

In the quiet corners of their minds, many individuals grapple with the suffocating weight of guilt and shame instilled by church teachings on tithing. Sarah, a devoted member of her congregation for over a decade, recalls the swirl of anxiety that enveloped her every time the offering plate was passed. Each week, as she watched her peers eagerly contribute, her heart raced with a fear that seeped into her very being, creating a stark juxtaposition between her faith and her financial reality. Living paycheck to paycheck, Sarah often felt the piercing gaze of judgment from her fellow churchgoers, a feeling exacerbated by sermons that echoed warnings of impending curses for those who failed to tithe. The pastor's fervent words felt less like a gentle nudge towards generosity and more like a relentless hammer driving home the idea that her worthiness as a Christian hinged on her monetary contributions. As the pressure mounted, her spiritual life became an anxious labyrinth where self-worth was tied intricately to financial sacrifice, leading her to moments of despair when she could not meet the arbitrary benchmarks set by church leaders.

Jason, another congregant, experienced a similar ordeal. He could often recall how he would sit in the pew, heart thumping, as the speaker fervently urged the congregation to give ten percent, often backing his claims with selective scripture that left little room for doubt. For Jason, the crux of his torment lay in the unshakeable belief that he was being monitored, scrutinized not by God's grace but by the expectations of men. Feeling inadequate as a father and husband, he reluctantly dug into his savings to meet the demands, all the while knowing it was meant for other pressing needs in his family. This incessant give more approach left him feeling spiritually bankrupt and emotionally depleted, breeding resentment not just against his church but against the very faith that had once provided him solace. In his darkest hours, Jason struggled to reconcile his sense of devotion with the relentless feeling of being a failure in the eyes of his spiritual community. The weight of financial burdens colored his prayer life, where fear replaced faith, and despair overshadowed hope.

Then there was Mia, whose testimony echoed the sentiments of countless others who found the church's financial expectations crushing. After a particularly fiery sermon on wealth and blessings, Mia began experiencing physical manifestations of the psychological toll. Nightmares plagued her sleep, tormenting her with visions of financial ruin as her mind twisted the pastor's words into dire predictions of hardship and loss. Each time someone asked her about her church involvement, she flinched, bracing herself for the inevitable question about what percentage she was giving. The fear of ostracism grew so profound that Mia started distancing herself from friends who she believed would judge her for being less than generous. Once a vibrant and active member of her church, she found herself retreating into isolation, feeling as if her value was diminished to mere dollar signs. Each testimony like hers illuminated a deep-seated anxiety that emerged in the absence of understanding and compassion, where affection turned to fear, and community evolved into a source of pressure rather than a safe haven for exploration and growth.

These stories intertwine to paint a haunting portrait of a faith culture drenched in manipulation, where financial sacrifices overshadow grace, creating a chasm between the intended message of love and the grim reality of fear. The testimonies serve as testimonies to a broader systemic issue, revealing the deeply entrenched belief that one's relationship with God is directly linked to their financial contributions, a notion that not only distorts the essence of faith but also leaves lasting scars on the mental health and spiritual well-being of those ensnared by such beliefs. As more voices join in the chorus of dissent against these practices, the hope for a transformative shift in the narrative around tithing and spiritual giving becomes ever more palpable, igniting a seed of inquiry that seeks to liberate individuals from the chains of guilt, shame, and fear that have long dictated their spiritual journeys.

The Burden of Guilt

In the shadows of church pews, a palpable weight often lingers, weaving itself into the very fabric of devotion: the burden of guilt. For many followers of Christ, the teachings surrounding tithing extend far beyond mere financial contributions; they morph into an oppressive shroud, casting a long shadow over their spiritual well-being. The testimonies of individuals wrestling with the emotional fallout from these enforced teachings reveal a relentless cycle of shame and inadequacy, feelings that seem to seep into their very identities. Imagine sitting in a sanctuary filled with worshippers, yet feeling isolated within one's own thoughts, the pastor's voice ringing clearly about the necessity of tithing, laced with dire warnings of curses awaiting those who falter in their financial loyalties. The narratives emerge as haunting reflections, where personal faith becomes entwined with fear, painting a scenario where financial figures eclipse the message of grace and love that religion is meant to embody.

One individual, Sarah, shares her journey through a labyrinth of anxiety; she recalls the sermons where she felt as if each word targeted her directly, the pastor's impassioned pleas hitting her like a relentless drumbeat. "If I didn't meet my tithing obligations, not only was I letting my church down, but I was also risking God's displeasure," she reflects, her words filled with a tremor of remembering. It was not just a matter of money; it became an internal struggle that pitted her against an unwinnable dichotomy of faithfulness and financial fidelity. Each time the offering plate passed her by, the rush of shame surged like a tide, an all-consuming reminder of her perceived shortcomings. "I found myself calculating every dollar—should I buy groceries or give that $50 I had left to the church?" she confesses, her eyes glassy with the memories of weighing her financial situation against her spiritual obligations.

Another testimony surfaces from Paul, a man who once thrived in his career until the church's teachings locked him in a cage of self-doubt and fear of failure. He explains the mental health repercussions of believing oneself cursed for not giving enough. "I remember feeling like I was walking on eggshells every time we discussed finances; I was terrified of sharing my true struggles." The guilt morphed into an insidious anxiety that lurked in the background of his daily life. Paul recalls how the constant mental chatter of inadequacy affected his relationships, strained his marriage, and even clouded his connection with God. He explains, "The church's narrative made me feel like my worth was tied to my wallet, and when I couldn't measure up, it felt like I was being cast away." This poignant insight reveals an essential truth about the human experience under the weight of guilt; instead of fostering a supportive community, these teachings can fracture relationships and twist the notion of faith into something transactional and empty.

As we peel back the layers of these experiences, it becomes clear that the ramifications of tithing-related guilt extend far beyond individual psyches. These emotions sow seeds of distrust not only in one's relationship with financial stewardship but also in their fundamental relationship with faith itself. For many, the concept of God transforms from a source of unconditional love and compassion to a figure of judgment, measuring their worthiness by their financial contributions. The tragic irony lies in the fact that the principles of generosity and compassion that should be woven into the fabric of faith become distorted into a ledger of compliance and condemnation. Moreover, the accounts presented are often devoid of acknowledgment of the diverse financial landscapes in which followers of Christ find themselves, ignoring the complexities of individual circumstances and the myriad of challenges one may face.

In understanding the visceral repercussions of guilt tethered to tithing practices, we unearth the necessity for compassion and a more profound understanding of what it means to walk in faith. The burden should not be one of shame and fear but rather an opportunity for community and connection, fostering an atmosphere where love can flourish without the threat of judgment. Hence, examining the phenomenon of guilt associated with tithing calls for a movement away from fear-driven practices toward a renewed approach rooted in generosity and grace, where individuals can feel free to engage with their faith without feeling diminished by financial constraints. The road ahead invites us as a community to challenge these oppressive teachings and envision a future steeped in compassion, where the tenets of faith do not burden the soul but uplift it, allowing for a holistic exploration of what it means to give—not out of fear, but from a place of love and abundance.

The Search for Acceptance

Many individuals' seeking acceptance within their religious communities find themselves ensnared in the web of tithing, a practice that has been marketed as a pathway to spiritual validation and divine favor. It is a deeply ingrained belief in many churches that to please God, one must generously give ten percent of their income, and for many, failing to meet this expectation becomes a source of profound guilt and shame. Testimonies abound from followers of Christ who have felt the heavy mantle of financial obligation weighing upon them, leading to an internal struggle that extends far beyond monetary concerns. The fear of being perceived as less faithful or inadequate by their peers often translates into an overwhelming pressure to conform, with many drowning in self-doubt over their spiritual worthiness. Stories echo in church hallways of those who, despite stretching their finances beyond reasonable limits, experienced the disheartening sensation of never doing enough in the eyes of God or their leaders. This relentless pursuit of validation through tithing creates a cycle where individuals become trapped in their desire for acceptance — a sort of spiritual hamster wheel, where they keep running but never move forward.

The ramifications of this pursuit are significant. Mental health issues such as anxiety and depression can take root, borne from the relentless fear of financial ruin or even divine disfavor tied to their inability to contribute monetarily in the prescribed manner. Some recount laying awake at night, trembling under the weight of the perceived curses that could befall them for not adhering to the church's teachings. In these vulnerable moments, the church's messages transform into a haunting lullaby of worry that lingers throughout their day-to-day lives, affecting relationships, self-esteem, and even their ability to fully embrace their faith. For some, the fear becomes so pervasive that it leads to financial decisions that compromise their basic wellbeing, as they choose to prioritize tithing over essential needs like food, healthcare, or education. The testimonies reveal a troubling pattern where individuals inadvertently equate their value to their monetary contributions, leading to a distorted view of their relationship with their faith and God. The church, a designated space for spiritual growth and encouragement, becomes instead a stage for the performance of financial metrics, where those who cannot keep up feel diminished. This creates a culture rife with comparison, where members gauge their spirituality based on their financial sacrifices rather than their inherent value as children of God.

Ultimately, it begs the question: at what cost does this search for acceptance come? The pursuit of financial validation within the church framework can lead to a disconnect from the true essence of faith — an understanding that grace, love, and acceptance are fundamental tenets that require neither payment nor performance. The need to fit into a pre-defined mold of what it means to be a "good Christian" based on financial stature traps many in a cycle of emotional turmoil, threatening to erode the very community they yearn to belong to. The stories serve as poignant reminders of the complexity of human emotion and our innate desire to be valued not for what we can give, but for who we are. As we unravel these narratives, it becomes increasingly critical to recognize that acceptance should stem from love and understanding, rather than fear, and in acknowledging this, we pave the way for a more inclusive, compassionate, and genuinely supportive church environment.

Chapter Five

Alternatives to Tithing

Voluntary Giving

In a landscape where financial contributions to churches are often entwined with the heavy chain of obligation, the notion of voluntary giving stands as a liberating alternative, inviting followers of Christ to share their resources based not on compulsion but rather on personal conviction and genuine desire to support their community. Imagine a church environment where the ethos revolves around the encouraging vibrancy of generosity; a space where individuals genuinely feel inspired to contribute, know their gifts will be used wisely, and understand that their participation is not just expected but celebrated. This paradigm shift requires a fundamental rethinking of how we approach church funding, moving away from fear-based tactics to a model founded on trust, transparency, and shared values. The beauty of voluntary giving lies in its capacity to foster a profound sense of community and connection. When individuals contribute because they choose to, rather than because they are coerced into it or paralyzed by the fear of financial repercussions, the entire act transforms into a collective expression of faith and abundance rather than a mere obligation satisfied to avoid guilt or consequences.

Through community-supported initiatives, followers of Christ can pool resources for projects that genuinely resonate with them, enriching their spiritual lives and fostering deeper relationships with one another. These initiatives could encompass everything from providing greater assistance to local charities, funding community missions, or supporting church activities that promote engagement and spiritual growth. Volunteerism also plays an essential role in this new approach to church funding. When individuals offer their skills, time, and expertise freely, they contribute in ways that go beyond financial support, enriching the church's efforts with their passion and commitment. This calling, rather than an additional burden, becomes a joyful act of service, where members feel valued and integral to the church's mission. Consequently, as more followers of Christ embrace the freedom of giving willingly and cheerfully, the entire church is likely to flourish, basking in the generosity of its members motivated by love and appreciation instead of fear and obligation.

Moreover, embracing voluntary giving can help cultivate a culture of transparency between church leaders and their congregations. When church finances are presented openly, highlighting how every donation is utilized for the betterment of both the community and its members, individuals are more inclined to trust their leaders and believe in the shared vision. This transparency fosters accountability, sparking constructive dialogue about financial ethics and promoting stewardship practices that align with the church's values. It encourages followers of Christ to actively participate in discussions surrounding the church's financial decisions rather than remaining passive recipients of information. As trust deepens, individuals become not just financial supporters but active partners, forging an authentic bond with the mission of the church as they witness their contributions making a tangible difference in the lives of others. In this encouraging atmosphere, the conversation about money and faith transforms into one characterized by hope, collaboration, and shared responsibility, dismantling the specter of manipulation that too often looms large over the contemporary church's approach to funding.

Ultimately, the ministry that thrives on voluntary giving is imbued with a genuine sense of purpose. When individuals give what they can afford to, motivated by love and community spirit, it enriches not only the financial health of the church but nurtures the spiritual well-being of its members. This model stands in stark contrast to manipulative systems that push individuals to meet arbitrary financial quotas. In this nurturing environment, the fabric of relationships is strengthened as followers of Christ witness their impact, creating a virtuous cycle of generosity that becomes infectious. The joy of giving, rooted in personal belief and unconditional support for the community, flows freely, creating lasting bonds that transcend mere financial transactions and turn into meaningful partnerships in faith. It is the exploration of this alternative path to church funding that invites readers to reclaim their relationship with money and faith, invoking a sense of empowerment that profoundly redefines the landscape of their spiritual journeys.

Community Support

In exploring models of community-funded churches, it becomes increasingly evident that the essence of church funding can thrive on relationships built around generosity rather than obligation. Imagine a church where the congregation gathers not out of fear of curses for failing to tithe, but out of a shared vision of supporting one another and promoting collective welfare. Communities that adopt this philosophy embrace a tapestry of support woven through voluntary giving, where contributions flourish organically, fueled by personal conviction and authentic connection with one another. In these models, the emphasis shifts from a rigid percentage of income mandated as a tithe to participatory approaches that invite every member to contribute in ways that resonate with their individual passions and resources. This can manifest in many forms—be it financial donations, time volunteered for outreach programs, or skills offered to enhance church activities—each an offering of love and service that reflects the spirit of community engagement. The power of building financial underpinnings in this manner cannot be understated; it fosters an environment where every contributor feels valued, appreciated, and integral to the community's mission. By encouraging open dialogues about finances—discussions that inspire full transparency regarding how funds are raised and allocated—congregations can build trust and accountability, dismantling any fears rooted in secrecy or manipulation. Such open discussions can lead to innovative fundraising initiatives, including community events that not only generate support but also strengthen relationships among members, reinforcing the belief that the church is not merely a building but a living, breathing community of believers. In these environments, the act of giving transforms into an expression of love and commitment to shared values, displacing the notion that one's relationship with God hinges on fulfilling a monetary obligation. By highlighting models of community-funded churches, we can envision a reformation in how financial contributions are perceived, where the ultimate goal is no longer about meeting a quota but nurturing a fellowship built on mutual support, compassion, and the buoyancy of shared faith. It becomes a collective mission where, rather than feeling like an isolated individual compelled to contribute out of fear, each member acts as part of a vibrant community knitted together by a tapestry of selfless generosity, thus redefining the relationship between faith and finances in a truly liberating manner.

Transparency in Church Finances

In the evolving landscape of modern spirituality, the need for transparency in church finances cannot be overstated. Communities thrive on trust, and when followers of Christ feel left in the dark about how their contributions are utilized, it breeds skepticism and resentment. Imagine a church environment where open discussions about budgets, expenditures, and financial priorities become the norm rather than the exception; a place where every member knows not only how much the church collects but also how those funds are allocated to serve the community, support local initiatives, or contribute to broader missions beyond the church walls. Such transparency fosters a culture of accountability, where church leaders are expected to justify their financial decisions and empower the congregation to actively participate in the dialogue. This shift from secrecy to openness encourages parishioners to reflect on their financial commitments, inspiring them to give based on genuine enthusiasm and personal conviction rather than pressure or fear. Moreover, by adopting community-supported models and volunteer-driven projects, churches can tap into the innate generosity within their congregations, creating pathways for individuals to contribute in ways that align with their values and life circumstances. In this environment of shared responsibility and altruism, financial discussions can lead to collaborative decision-making, where members are not just passive recipients of the church's vision but active contributors, crafting initiatives that resonate with their beliefs and experiences. As churches adopt clearer financial practices, they reclaim the narrative from manipulation to empowerment, inviting followers of Christ to invest in a shared mission and experience the transformation that comes when finances are rooted in community and transparency rather than obligation. This model not only teaches responsible stewardship but also embeds a sense of belonging that reflects the true essence

of faith—love, generosity, and shared purpose—
ultimately leading to a more vibrant, engaged,
and committed congregation.

Chapter Six

The Case Against Tithing

Financial Manipulation

In the heart of many modern churches, a troubling reality unfolds—financial manipulation disguised as holy obligation. The practice of tithing, once a mere fragment of ancient Judah's religious structure, has evolved into a powerful tool for financial gain that church leaders wield to ensure a steady stream of income into their institutions. It is a paradox, a systematic contradiction when analyzed through the lenses of ethics and spirituality, for what began as a voluntary surrender of one-tenth of one's produce has morphed into an insidious demand that can paralyze the faithful with fear and anxiety. Theologians and financial experts alike have begun to scrutinize the mechanics of this transformation, exposing the layers of manipulation that often go unnoticed as followers of Christ dutifully drop their checks into offering plates with unwavering belief in their own starry-eyed faithful service. According to many testimonies provided by former church members who have extracted themselves from these entanglements, the overwhelming pressure to meet tithing expectations creates a dangerous environment where spiritual life and financial well-being become intertwined to the point that individuals find it increasingly difficult to separate the promise of eternal salvation from their monetary contributions. Incessant sermons ringing out about the blessings that come from tithing, paired with anecdotes of financial misfortune befalling non-tithers, cultivate an atmosphere where guilt and fear reign supreme, compelling individuals to keep giving despite the financial strain that they may be experiencing in their own lives. These manipulative strategies not only compromise the integrity of the congregation's purpose but undeniably skew the sacred relationship between faith and finances. When church leaders architect financial models based on culpability—selectively interpreting scripture and crafting narratives that promise divine recompense for sacrificial giving—it is the individual followers of Christ who bare the burdens, often leading to a cycle of debt, desperation, and shattered trust. Thus, the conversation must shift; we need to question whether the modernization of tithing as a forced obligation, masked by spiritual rhetoric, is ethical and whether it serves the community of believers or the financial ambitions of the church itself. The ethical dilemmas posed by these practices call for an urgent re-examination of faith, finance, and the intended freedom that the spiritual journey is meant to embody. This is an appeal for transparency—one that champions community support over coercive compliance, advocating for a generous spirit that flourishes in an atmosphere of love rather than fear. Advocating for voluntary giving is not just a rallying cry for financial liberation; it transforms the very foundations of faith-based giving and reshapes the personal relationships followers of Christ have with their communities and their Creator, allowing them to approach spiritual life with an open heart rather than one shackled by unrelenting guilt and financial strain.

The Ethics of Giving

In examining the ethics of giving, the practice of mandatory tithing emerges as a deeply controversial topic that raises significant moral questions about the relationship between faith, finance, and the power dynamics within church communities. Tithing, originally tied to the ancient covenant between God and a specific people, transforms in contemporary settings, often becoming less about spiritual obligation and more about institutional gain. The testimonies of former followers of Christ echo throughout the discourse, revealing how coercive financial demands can lead to feelings of guilt and fear rather than joy and gratitude. Theologians, who analyze the scriptural foundations of tithing, also note that within the

New Testament, there is a marked shift toward voluntary giving, which emphasizes the spirit of generosity over mandated contributions. Financial experts contribute their insights, pointing to the psychological effects of mandatory tithing on individuals' well-being and financial health. Many former members recount stories of financial strain, where families are pressured to commit a portion of their income to the church, often at the expense of their basic needs or savings for emergencies. This practice raises questions: In what way does a church serve its community by demanding financial sacrifice, especially when it could prioritize compassion and understanding in economic hardship? The act of giving, ideally born out of love and commitment, becomes entangled in a web of ethical conundrums when tied to threats of divine retribution or fear of community exclusion. Moreover, the lack of transparency in church finances only exacerbates these ethical dilemmas; without clarity regarding how funds are allocated or spent, followers of Christ may feel misled or exploited. It is imperative to question whether encouraging financial contributions through compliance reflects the heart of a faith community or betrays the core principles of love, generosity, and mutual support that many religious teachings espouse. These reflections compel us to consider not only the intent behind giving but also the broader implications of fostering a culture where giving is coerced rather than voluntary, leading to a foundational reevaluation of how churches engage with their faithful, and a necessary dialogue about the moral responsibilities both on the part of the church and its members in fostering a more ethical approach to financial stewardship.

Real Stories of Struggle

In the quiet corners of many congregations, beneath the surface of polished sermons and uplifting music, lie real stories of struggle— narratives filled with tears, sleepless nights, and the gnawing anxiety that comes from making ends meet. Among those who have faced the relentless pressure to tithe, individuals often recount the discomfort of forgoing their basic needs in service of what they believed was a divine mandate. Take, for instance, Sarah, a single mother who found herself in a vicious cycle, trapped between the demands of her church and the reality of her finances. Each month, she would tithe faithfully, as the pastor urged his congregation that failing to do so would invite misfortune. With every check she wrote, she felt the weight of expectation bearing down on her, leading to choices that left her family in precarious situations—balancing on the razor's edge between hunger and faith. Similarly, there was James, a once-enthusiastic member of a thriving evangelical community, whose commitment to tithing swiftly escalated into a source of shame as he faced unemployment. Each Sunday felt like a reckoning, with his pastor's fervent reminders echoing in his mind while his bank account dwindled to alarming lows. He would sit in the pew, battling inner turmoil, knowing he should support the church but feeling the pang of guilt for not being able to provide enough for his own household. The struggle was not just financial; it manifested into a crisis of faith, as he questioned whether devotion required such sacrifice. These stories, shared by many individuals navigating the treacherous waters of financial obligation to their churches, reveal a troubling reality wherein the sacred act of worship becomes intertwined with the stress of economic survival. With debts mounting and moral dilemmas lurking in every decision, followers of Christ often wrestle with loyalty to their faith while simultaneously confronting the ethical implications of those demanding their hard-earned money. This tension not only erodes personal relationships but also disturbs the very fabric of community, where individuals like Sarah and James grapple with the dichotomy of giving as an act of love and the painful reminder of scarcity that the church's teachings reluctantly impose. Financial experts and theologians alike have highlighted this trend, arguing that churches, as stewards of faith, should prioritize the well-being of their followers of Christ over the bottom line, promoting a culture of generosity rather than one of guilt. As these real stories emerge, they illustrate a pressing need for reform within religious institutions, fostering transparency and compassion rather than manipulation—creating a space where giving is driven by love and not obligation.

Chapter Seven

Reclaiming Financial Freedom

Budgeting Tips

In reclaiming financial autonomy, it is essential to approach budgeting with clarity and intent. Begin by assessing your current financial situation; take a deep dive into your income sources, expenses, and any debt you may have accumulated. It can be a liberating experience, akin to unveiling a hidden truth about your financial landscape. Create a visual representation, such as a spreadsheet or a simple app, to categorize your monthly income and expenses. Identify essentials versus non-essentials, distinguishing between what you need to live and what brings you joy, ensuring you allocate funds to both without guilt. Setting financial goals is equally paramount; whether it is saving for a vacation, a new car, or simply for a rainy day, having clear objectives can motivate you to stick to your budget. Next, prioritize your spending by adjusting your lifestyle gradually to align with your goals. Instead of feeling pressured to meet societal expectations, focus on what genuinely matters to you. This may mean enjoying free community events, dining out less frequently, or seeking alternative entertainment options that do not strain your finances. Remember to allocate some funds for aiding causes that resonate with you, reinforcing a sense of control over your contributions without obligatory tithing that may not reflect your values. Creating a separate donation fund allows you to support organizations you truly believe in, enhancing your connection to community and charity. Regularly review and adjust your budget, reflecting any changes in your financial circumstances or personal values. It's a continual journey toward greater financial literacy and empowerment; by actively engaging in positive budgeting practices, not only do you honor your financial commitments, but you also foster a healthy relationship with money— transforming it from a source of anxiety into a tool for abundance and joy. This proactive approach encourages an intentional rhythm, where each dollar is treated with respect and purpose, allowing you to break free from guilt and embrace the abundance of choice in how you spend, save, and give. Make the conscious choice to budget wisely, keeping your values at the forefront, and watch how your financial landscape begins to shift toward one of empowerment and generosity, free from the burdens typically associated with traditional tithing. As you cultivate this newfound relationship with money, take the time to reflect on how your financial practices align with your spiritual journey; seek to create an environment where your giving stems from a place of love and joy, not fear or obligation, thus redefining your role in the community and your heart.

Choosing Where to Give

When it comes to choosing where to give, the journey begins with a heart-engaged reflection on personal values and passions. It is essential to break free from the guilt and perceived obligation that often accompany the practice of traditional tithing, allowing oneself the clarity to reclaim financial autonomy. Imagine the resources you have at your disposal not as a burden or a necessary chore but as a remarkable opportunity to impact the world in a way that resonates with your own beliefs. Sit down with a pen and paper or open up your digital notepad, and make a list of the causes that genuinely speak to your soul—be it education, health care, environmental conservation, social justice, or support for local homeless shelters. The moment you align your giving with your passions, you reclaim the narrative around your finances, transforming the sordid history of obligation into a vibrant expression of generosity.

As you navigate your financial landscape, start budgeting with intention and thoughtfulness to identify how much you can give comfortably without feeling strained or anxious. This might involve taking a closer look at your spending habits, recognizing areas where you can cut back, allowing you to redirect those funds to initiatives that matter to you. Embrace the idea that giving does not always have to be a grand act; even small contributions to your cherished causes, cumulatively over time, can lead to substantial change. It is about being engaged and thoughtful, stepping away from the mechanized, guilt-ridden approach to tithing so often propagated by institutional constructs. By choosing where to give with discernment, not only do you foster a healthy relationship with money, but you also cultivate a deeper connection with your community and the world at large.

Moreover, consider finding organizations or causes that embody the values you hold dear, and research their missions, leadership, and impact. Ask questions about how your contributions are used—this creates an environment of transparency and trust. If you are drawn to a local charity, volunteer your time in addition to monetary support; this allows for a more profound relationship with the cause, fostering community ties that extend beyond financial transactions. This engagement reinforces the idea that giving is a holistic experience, intertwining our lives with those we seek to uplift, thus deepening the importance of our contributions.

In this conscious approach to giving, make it a point to revisit your donation strategy periodically. As your life evolves, your passions may shift, and your priorities might expand. Whether that means developing an affinity for supporting youth education initiatives or investing in sustainable businesses, ensuring your contributions reflect your current values keeps the practice fluid and fulfilling. Ultimately, choosing where to give should be a liberating experience that ignites a sense of purpose and joy rather than fear or guilt, enriching both your life and the lives of others.

Building Financial Literacy

Understanding personal finance is crucial for anyone seeking to break the chains of guilt associated with tithing, and it serves as a vital steppingstone toward reclaiming financial autonomy. To embark on this journey, one must first grasp the foundational principles of budgeting. This involves not only tracking income and expenses but also comprehending the underlying flow of money in and out of one's life. Creating a budget is not merely a task; it is a profound act of self-reflection and tomorrow's planning, allowing individuals to visualize their spending habits and understand where they can adjust without causing emotional upheaval. A well-structured budget can illuminate opportunities for savings and discretionary spending, presenting possibilities for directing funds toward causes that resonate personally, instead of yielding to guilt-fueled obligations.

When individuals start allocating funds toward causes they care about, a shift in mindset often occurs, replacing feelings of resentment or obligation with joy and purpose. This practice not only enriches the experience of giving but also nurtures a healthy relationship with money—one built on values and personal convictions rather than fear of repercussions or societal pressures. By taking charge of their financial situation, people can cultivate an appreciation for their ability to choose where their money flows, reinforcing their autonomy and fostering a sense of empowerment. It is essential to view money not as a master that dictates life choices, but rather as a tool—a means to fulfill aspirations and support missions that align with one's beliefs.

Moreover, engaging in educational resources related to financial literacy further enhances this journey. There are numerous books, podcasts, and workshops designed to enlighten anyone willing to learn. They dissect intricate financial concepts into relatable, digestible insights that lay the groundwork for making wiser financial decisions. By empowering oneself with knowledge, individuals can confront the realities of their financial landscape, shape a future that reflects their true values, and break free from the cycle of guilt associated with traditional expectations of giving. Ultimately, building financial literacy is not merely about mastering numbers; it is about fostering a harmonious relationship with money, one that reflects newfound confidence and liberates individuals from outdated beliefs, opening the door to a future filled with hope and generosity motivated by the heart.

Chapter Eight

A New Paradigm for Giving

Love Offerings

In contemplating the essence of giving within the church, one must redirect the focus from mere obligation to the profound expression of love that exists in the act of generosity. This shift towards love offerings signifies not only a departure from the restrictive notions that often ensnare followers of Christ but also embodies a celebration of community and shared purpose. Love offerings give individuals the opportunity to give freely, prompted by genuine gratitude and a desire to support the spiritual home that nurtures their faith journey, rather than feeling coerced into compliance with an outdated mandate. It is essential to foster an environment where contributions are a reflection of personal conviction and heartfelt desire, allowing each member of the community to express their support in a way that resonates with their personal relationships with God.

Imagine a congregation where the act of giving is infused with the warmth of love, where individuals eagerly contribute their resources because they recognize the deep connection between their financial gifts and the broader ministry that serves their community's needs.

Picture bustling gatherings where church members come together not merely to meet a numerical quota but to engage, inspire, and uplift one another through the joy of generosity. In this transformed space, the spirit of giving becomes a natural overflow of gratitude, flowing from hearts that are attuned to the needs of others and the mission set forth by the church. This model embraces creativity and flexibility, celebrating the many forms that love offerings can take—perhaps it is a generous donation, a homemade meal shared during community events, or volunteering time and talents to achieve a common goal. By moving away from rote calculations of a fixed percentage, followers of Christ can craft their unique narrative of giving, one that aligns with their values and circumstances, nurturing a culture brimming with mutual support and kindness.

The impact of love offerings extends beyond mere financial assistance; it fosters a sense of belonging, belongingness, and emotional investment within the church community. Members become increasingly engaged when they perceive their contributions as meaningful, especially when encouraged to participate in decisions regarding how those resources are channeled for the benefit of the broader community. This collaborative approach invites followers of Christ into an open dialogue about the church's needs, aspirations, and financial stewardship. It compels them to take ownership of the church's direction and objectives, cultivating an atmosphere of trust that invigorates the spiritual fabric of the community. As individuals witness the tangible outcomes of their generosity—a new outreach initiative, improved facilities that serve the community better, or social programs that alleviate poverty—they find not only satisfaction in their personal giving but also a shared pride illuminating the church's mission.

When the act of giving is tethered to love rather than obligation, congregations stand to flourish without the shadows of financial pressure looming overhead. The traditional notion of tithing can stifle creativity and deter participation; however, by embracing a model centered on love offerings, churches liberate their members from anxiety and fear, allowing for a more organic and heartfelt engagement with the ministry. In this new paradigm, generosity becomes an everyday practice, a way of life that is comfortably woven into the fabric of each member's spiritual walk. The joy derived from such sincere acts serves to elevate the overall church experience, transforming not just the financial framework of the congregation but invigorating its mission to spread love and hope. Imagine a landscape where giving is a true joy and a celebration, a collective effort reflecting the light of Christ's love in the world, unburdened by external pressures and rooted deeply in the nurturing soil of a community committed to caring for one another, all sparked by the spirit of love offerings.

Community Engagement

In reimagining church funding, the power of community engagement emerges as a transformative force, instilling a sense of belonging and mutual support among followers of Christ that transcends mere financial transactions. This model advocates for a shift from obligatory tithing, often steeped in guilt and fear, to a more organic approach where each individual's contributions are an expression of gratitude and love towards their community. Understanding that the strength of a church lies not solely in its financial wealth, but rather in the warmth of relationships built upon genuine commitment to one another, fosters an environment where fellowship thrives. Rather than each member feeling the weight of a mandated percentage, followers of Christ can freely offer their resources—whether time, talent, or treasures—in whatever form they choose, thus creating a tapestry of support that reflects the diverse gifts within the body of Christ.

Imagine a church where community engagement is not just encouraged but celebrated, where members collaborate on local initiatives that address real needs and challenges. In this atmosphere, volunteer efforts transform lives, as individuals come together to support local families in crisis, provide meals for the hungry, mentor youth, or create safe spaces for various groups. These acts of service are a manifestation of the collective spirit within the church, and the resulting energy cultivates deeper connections between members and their wider community. As relationships strengthen, so does the church's relevance, becoming a beacon of hope, a source of solidarity in challenging times, and a hub for collaborative endeavors that extend beyond the church walls.

Moreover, this engagement fosters transparency in financial matters, as the lines between giving and receiving blur in a healthy symbiotic relationship. When contributions come freely, without coercion, there is an inherent understanding that every offering is a choice made from the heart—whether it's a love offering to support a family in need, donating supplies for a community project, or simply participating in fundraisers with joyous hearts. Rather than focusing solely on budgets and quotas, church leaders can direct their attention to nurturing relationships, ensuring that every person feels seen, valued, and integral to the mission of the church. This collective participation in community and supportive practices not only empowers the followers of Christ but also flourishes into an enriching experience that resonates beyond the church and into the communities surrounding it.

Under this new paradigm, the narrative shifts from one of obligation to one of ecstatic affirmation of faith, as members witness the tangible impact of their shared resources producing real change. The joy of giving transforms into a personal celebration—an opportunity to express love not only to the church community but also to the broader society. Encouraging followers of Christ to see their actions—be it kindness, service, or financial support—as ways to reflect their faith leads to a new culture of generosity. This culture can inspire a legacy of giving that prolongs beyond one's lifetime as members band together, rooted in purpose, spurring one another on to increase their efforts in both service and giving, resulting in a cycle of blessing that never ceases to flow. In this way, church funding becomes not an isolated act, but a communal response, rendering manifestations of faith that affirm the call to love your neighbor as yourself, and become a powerful testimony to the life-changing potential of the church when it fully engages with its community.

Rethinking Church Finances

Rethinking church finances involves a transformative approach that prioritizes the genuine spirit of generosity over obligatory giving and fear-based mandates. This new model encourages churches to foster a culture where financial contributions stem from love offerings and voluntary participation rather than a sense of compulsion instilled by rigid tithing practices. In this paradigm, congregations are invited to engage in open discussions about funding, creating a transparent atmosphere where members understand the financial needs of their church and feel empowered to contribute according to their means and personal convictions. The potential for flourishing congregations lies in recognizing that giving should be an act of joy and gratitude, an expression of faith and community rather than a compliance to an outdated obligation. By leaning into voluntary contributions, churches can organize events that invite members to participate in collective fundraising efforts that align with the mission and vision of the community, thereby fostering relationships based on trust and shared purpose.

Moreover, this new financial model can help demystify the use of church funds, making it imperative that leaders practice transparency and accountability regarding budgeting and expenditures. Educating followers of Christ on the church's financial endeavors can create a sense of ownership and pride among members, encouraging them to see their contributions as investments in the collective mission rather than mere transactions. This engagement can also extend beyond financial support, prompting church communities to explore alternative forms of giving, such as volunteering time and talents to enhance church programs or outreach initiatives. When followers of Christ see their involvement resulting in palpable impacts on their community, a natural cycle of motivation and generosity unfolds, encouraging others to join in and contribute in diverse ways.

This shift in mindset calls for churches to become less focused on maintaining financial structures built on fear of consequences for failing to give and more centered on cultivating an environment of mutual support and love. Church leaders should model this behavior by sharing stories of generosity, celebrating acts of giving, and expressing gratitude for all contributions received, regardless of their size. Implementing initiatives that promote service projects can draw members together in profound ways, solidifying community bonds that extend far beyond the walls of the church. These actions can manifest in volunteer days, community service events, or collaborative projects with local organizations, highlighting the power of working together to address communal needs, thereby reinforcing that the church's mission extends beyond its financial considerations.

In essence, the reimagining of church finances should emphasize relationship-building, vulnerability, and authenticity—fostering an environment where both leaders and followers of Christ can express their hopes, dreams, and financial challenges without fear or judgment. As this culture of generosity takes root, it can inspire creativity in addressing financial needs, leading to innovative solutions like community fundraisers, collaborations with local businesses or nonprofits, and the exploration of alternative funding sources. Through this lens, churches can not only thrive financially but also spiritually, as followers of Christ rally around a shared mission of love, service, and support, illuminating a path towards financial freedom that harmonizes faith and community engagement in a way that uplifts all involved.

Chapter Nine

Empowering the Congregation

Questions to Ask Leadership

In the complex landscape of church finance, it becomes imperative for followers of Christ to be not just passive recipients of teachings but active participants, particularly when it comes to understanding how their contributions are utilized. Engaging with church leadership about financial practices should not be a mere exercise in checking off a list of questions; rather, it should serve as a dialogue that fosters mutual respect, clarity, and accountability. One of the most profound yet often overlooked aspects of church membership is the power of inquiry, and followers of Christ should not shy away from asking pointed, thoughtful questions that will shed light on the intricate workings of church finances. When approaching your church leaders, it can be helpful to begin with inquiries surrounding the overall financial health of the congregation. Questions like, "Can you share a detailed breakdown of our annual budget, including allocations for staff salaries, building maintenance, and outreach programs?" can in effect open a dialogue that encourages transparency. Furthermore, asking about the church's financial policies regarding tithes and offerings can help clarify whether these funds are being used to support the church community in tangible ways or if they are simply funneled into a system that may operate behind closed doors. Additionally, exploring the motivations and expectations surrounding tithing can shift the conversation toward more spiritual and ethical considerations. For instance, asking, "What teachings underpin our practice of tithing, and how do we ensure these teachings align with the message of love and generosity that Jesus preached?" paves the way for a more profound reflection that may lead both leaders and followers of Christ to reassess the true essence of their financial commitments. It is also key to question the church's stance on financial accountability—"What mechanisms are in place to monitor spending and ensure the money we contribute is being used ethically and responsibly?"—can not only shine a light on the church's processes but also invite leaders to reflect on their accountability measures to their congregation. There may be a need to inquire about how the church addresses financial difficulties, such as, "In times of budget shortfalls or unforeseen expenses, what steps the church might take to communicate these challenges to us, and how can we, as members, assist in navigating these difficulties?" Moreover, it could be potent to ask about the inclusion of followers of Christ in financial decisions. Questions like, "How can members get more involved in discussions regarding budget and allocation of funds?" or "Do we have financial committees that allow congregant input on financial matters?" can emphasize a desire for communal engagement and elucidate paths toward a participatory model. As you engage your church leaders with these profound questions, remember that the ultimate goal is a collaborative and open congregation where financial practices reflect the values of honesty, generosity, and faithfulness, thereby inspiring a culture built on trust rather than fear or obligation. Your willingness to inquire, seek clarity, and engage openly with church leadership not only empowers you but also plants the seeds for a culture of financial transparency within your church that can lead to greater spiritual freedom for all members of the community.

Building a Support Network

Building a support network around financial concerns in the church community is essential for fostering transparency, accountability, and an environment where open discussions can flourish. Imagine gathering with a small group of fellow followers of Christ who share your desire for clarity regarding the church's financial practices. This informal coalition can serve as a safe space where members can voice their questions and concerns, creating a sense of camaraderie and shared purpose. As you share your anecdotes and experiences, you will discover that others have similarly felt puzzlement or unease about the financial expectations set forth by leadership. Engaging in these discussions can not only reassure individuals who might feel isolated in their apprehensions but also empower the group as you collectively seek answers and clarity. To facilitate these conversations, consider organizing regular meetups that allow for an exchange of ideas and strategies; whether it is a coffee gathering after church, a weekly discussion group, or even a dedicated online forum, the opportunities are endless. Within this network, emphasize the importance of approaching church leaders collaboratively rather than confrontationally, framing inquiries about financial practices as a pursuit of shared wisdom rather than a challenge to authority. When questions arise, members can rally together, presenting their inquiries as a united front, thereby reducing the potential for backlash and fostering a spirit of unity. Moreover, forming connections with like-minded individuals can kindle new ideas about alternative contributions, allowing members to explore ways of giving that resonate with their values rather than adhering to outdated mandates. Ultimately, as individuals grow in their understanding of the church's financial practices, they also contribute to a culture of accountability, prompting leaders to be more forthcoming with information and encouraging a more ethical approach to church funding. In this way, the support network becomes not just a platform for voicing concerns but a transformative force that cultivates a community built on openness, respect, and genuine spiritual growth, paving the way for a more enlightened and empowered congregation.

Staying Informed

Financial literacy among church members is a vital aspect of fostering a more just and transparent financial environment within religious institutions. Understanding finances not only empowers followers of Christ to take an active role in discussions about church funding but also equips them with the knowledge needed to demand transparency and accountability from their leaders. Many individuals enter church communities with a sense of trust, often believing that their contributions will be used wisely and ethically. However, this trust can lead to complacency, which is detrimental when it comes to financial oversight. To combat this, church members must educate themselves about the financial practices and statements presented by their churches. Familiarity with budgeting, spending patterns, and revenue sources enables followers of Christ to engage meaningfully in conversations about the church's financial direction. Asking informed questions about how funds are allocated and requesting regular updates on church finances can instigate a healthier dialogue with church leadership.

It is essential for members to create a culture of inquiry, where financial discussions are seen as a necessary and integral part of communal life rather than a taboo topic cloaked in secrecy. This not only demystifies the financial operations of the church, but it also encourages leaders to maintain ethical stewardship of the resources entrusted to them by the congregation. Documenting questions and observations can also facilitate more structured conversations with church leaders. Those conversations might range from simple inquiries about specific expenditures to more complex discussions surrounding long-term financial planning and sustainability. Encouraging an environment where diverse voices can contribute to financial discussions ensures that multiple perspectives are considered, leading to more balanced decision-making.

Moreover, followers of Christ should seek to understand the broader implications of financial practices in their church community. For instance, examining how tithing affects the socioeconomic demographics of the congregation can yield insights into the potential for inclusivity or exclusivity prevalent in church practices. Engaging with financial literacy also means advocating for training sessions and workshops on personal finance, budgeting, and ethical giving within the church to elevate the entire congregation's understanding of financial stewardship. By building a foundation of financial knowledge, churches can cultivate a congregation that is both financially educated and spiritually empowered, capable of questioning and challenging potentially manipulative practices while fostering a more compassionate and collaborative approach to giving and generosity. This shift not only benefits individual members but also strengthens the community as a whole, reinforcing the idea that financial discussions should be open, constructive, and rooted in the shared goal of supporting the church's mission without yielding to fear or coercion. Ultimately, the more informed the congregation is, the better positioned they will be to contribute to a system that values transparency, accountability, and genuine stewardship of the resources that come from their collective sacrifices and goodwill.

Chapter Ten

The Future of Church Funding

Reforms in Church Funding

As we look toward a future where churches thrive on generosity rather than obligation, it becomes imperative to envision reforms in church funding that promote transparency, ethical stewardship, and community engagement. The foundation of these reforms should be built on a mutual understanding between church leaders and followers of Christ, fostering an atmosphere where financial discussions are not shrouded in secrecy or fear. One possible reform is to establish comprehensive financial education programs, equipping followers of Christ with the tools to understand church finances, including budgeting, giving, and the broader economic landscape they operate within. These programs could demystify how funds are utilized, showing followers of Christ the positive impacts of their generosity without imposing any metrics of obligation like tithing. In turn, this transparency could cultivate trust and a renewed sense of belonging, as members can witness firsthand the tangible outcomes of their contributions, such as community outreach, charity efforts, and support for local initiatives, which can be compelling motivators for voluntary generosity.

Moreover, churches could adopt a model of fundraising that prioritizes relational giving. By nurturing deep, authentic relationships within the community and emphasizing shared experiences and values over transactional relationships, churches can shift their paradigm from seeing followers of Christ merely as sources of revenue to recognizing them as integral partners in a shared mission. This model could focus on storytelling—a powerful tool in human connections—where church leaders and members share personal anecdotes about how internal contributions have transformed lives or facilitated community projects. Such narratives not only engage the congregation meaningfully but also build a culture that associates giving with love and passion rather than fear of withdrawal of blessings.

Additionally, churches might consider implementing a communal decision-making process regarding financial expenditures. Elected committees composed of congregation members could oversee budgets and spending plans, providing not just oversight but also a voice to diverse perspectives within the church. This shift would empower followers of Christ and foster a sense of ownership in the church's mission, breaking down the traditional top-down financial hierarchies and enhancing a collaborative spirit. As this spirit fosters deeper connections, it would naturally lead to a community built on shared investments rather than coerced contributions, enriching the church's character and outreach efforts profoundly.

Ultimately, these reforms seek to create healthier congregations and community relationships, where love and trust dismantle the structures of fear and manipulation that have too often characterized the practice of financial giving within churches. The call for change is not just about altering fiscal practices; it is a beckoning towards an entire cultural shift within religious communities. Envisioning a church landscape steeped in generosity and empowered decision-making is a crucial step toward realizing the collective potential of congregations and uplifting the spirit of giving to its most resplendent form. It is here, in this fertile ground of shared values and new practices, that the genuine essence of faith can flourish, unfettered from the chains of obligation and ushering forth a movement of liberty, generosity, and solidarity in the journey of faith.

A Vision for the Future

As we envision a future free from the heavy chains of coercive tithing practices, we must cultivate churches that embody principles of transparency, generosity, and community connection without the shadows of fear looming over their financial practices. Imagine congregations where every member feels valued not simply as contributors of funds but as integral parts of a holistic community working collaboratively towards shared missions. This shift could usher in healthier relationships between leaders and followers of Christ, restoring trust and mutual respect that may have been eroded by manipulative practices. By prioritizing open dialogues about financial matters, churches could embrace a model where stewardship is celebrated as a collective responsibility, rather than a pressure-laden obligation. Within such an environment, members would be free to give in ways that resonate with their beliefs and circumstances, nurturing a spirit of goodwill and voluntary support rather than the resentment that can fester under the weight of fear-based teachings.

Such a transition not only benefits the internal dynamics of churches, but it could also resonate outwardly, strengthening community ties. By engaging with local needs and projects, churches could become beacons of generosity and hope, leading initiatives that uplift those in distress, advocate for collective welfare, and provide support to the marginalized, thus truly embodying the essence of faith in action. When funding mechanisms shifts away from obligatory tithes to community-based support, we unlock a reservoir of creativity and commitment among church members eager to contribute without compulsion. This not only fosters positive mental health within congregations but also creates a vibrant culture of giving that reflects the diverse talents and resources possessed by its members. With a focus on collective goals, churches could lead by example, showcasing how the gospel message entails not just spiritual engagement but also a robust moral responsibility toward societal wellbeing.

In this reimagined future, we see a powerful synergy between financial ethics and spirituality, with churches taking bold steps to redefine what it means to be stewards of their resources. This could include establishing trusts or funds that transparently allocate donations towards mission-driven ventures instead of administrative costs or overly ambitious campaigns that prioritize profit over purpose. When congregations can leverage funds for meaningful impact, they will likely find members feeling a renewed sense of ownership and pride in their contributions. Moreover, the reduction of anxiety surrounding financial obligations could pave the way for deeper connections to the church's mission, allowing individuals to immerse themselves in spiritual growth, community engagement, and social justice initiatives with lighter hearts and open hands.

It is through this hopeful vision of the future that congregational life can reflect the true spirit of generosity, encouraging individuals to share abundantly and authentically without the specter of guilt or shame hovering over their decisions. In this context, financial discussions would become an integral part of church life, enriching the community's understanding of stewardship and collective responsibility rooted in love and transparency. The blend of financial stewardship and spiritual health becomes a powerful motivator for individuals to rethink their connections not only with their churches but also with their neighbors and the world at large. Such transformation will not come overnight; however, it begins with each person recognizing their power to influence change from within their congregations and advocating for a culture that values generosity over obligation. By building a future grounded in this hopeful vision, we can create spaces where faith and finances harmoniously coexist, nurturing both the soul and the community.

Creating a Culture of Giving

In the pursuit of a more liberated and rewarding spiritual experience, creating a culture of giving within churches can serve as a transformative catalyst that not only invigorates congregational life but also fosters a profound sense of community connection. Imagine a church environment where generosity flourishes naturally, where members are inspired to give freely, not out of fear or obligation, but from a deep-seated desire to support one another and contribute to the collective mission of love and service. In this vision, church leaders play a pivotal role in setting the tone, crafting messages that resonate with the human spirit's innate benevolence, rather than invoking guilt or impending doom for failing to meet financial obligations. By prioritizing stories of compassion and support over financial demands, leaders can shift the congregational mindset from one of scarcity to one of abundance, illustrating how shared resources and efforts can amplify the overall impact on the community. This approach not only builds trust but also cultivates an atmosphere where followers of Christ feel valued and empowered to contribute in ways that align with their personal convictions and financial capabilities. An effective strategy to reinforce this culture is through transparency in church finances, where followers of Christ are given clear insights into how funds are used, encouraging a deeper connection and sense of stewardship over shared resources. Workshops, discussions, and community service projects can be organized to highlight the joys and rewards that come from collective giving, showcasing how even small contributions can create immense change. Moreover, by highlighting personal testimonies of those beneficiaries of congregational generosity, churches can illuminate the tangible outcomes of giving, reinforcing the idea that every act of kindness adds to a legacy far beyond mere financial transactions. Cultivating an ethos of giving transforms the act from one of duty to one of joy and fulfillment, promoting spiritual growth and encouraging followers of Christ to view their financial contributions as investments in the broader mission of love and community outreach. As members witness the power of voluntary giving to uplift both the church and the surrounding community, they become ambassadors of generosity, inspiring others to embrace this mindset and creating a self-sustaining cycle of positive action and support. Ultimately, creating a culture of giving revolves around love, transparency, and mutual support, merging financial stewardship with spiritual fulfillment, thus paving the way for healthier, more vibrant congregations that thrive not in fear, but in the abundant grace of shared giving. In this nurturing environment, churches can break free from outdated manipulative practices, and instead, cultivate a movement of hope and collective benevolence that uplifts hearts and changes lives.

References

Tyndale. (2019). *NLT Life Application Study Bible, Third Edition*. Tyndale House Publishers, Inc.

Scripture quotations taken from The Holy Bible, New International Version, NIV. Copyright 1973, 1978, 1984, 2011 by Biblica, Inc.

Used by permission. All rights reserved worldwide.